INSPIRATION FROM GOD'S CREATION

Judith Asmus Hill

PublishAmerica
Baltimore

First printing

PublishAmerica has allowed this work to remain exactly as the author intended, verbatim, without editorial input.

Softcover 9781462689521
PUBLISHED BY PUBLISHAMERICA, LLLP
www.publishamerica.com
Baltimore

Printed in the United States of America

Contents

DEDICATION

I dedicate this third book of poetry to all those who are looking for God's inspiration in their everyday walk. Those who are seeking for answers to know God's will for their lives. I dedicate every poem and scripture to help encourage their hearts. Since the Holy Spirit teaches us many times through natural things, He then can give us "INSPIRATION FROM GOD'S CREATION!"

ACKNOWLEDGEMENTS

I would like to thank my precious Savior, Jesus Christ, who inspired me to write these poems & find passages from God's Word to bring help, healing & hope to every reader.

My heartfelt thanks to my wonderful husband, Jim, for his encouragement & help in every way to see that "INSPIRATION FROM GOD'S CREATION," came to fruition!

Jim & I would like to acknowledge & thank so many wonderful friends and family for all the prayers & hands on help that were given to my daughter Beth, during her many months of chemo and her surgeries & radiation to follow. This truly was an inspiration for me to hear God's voice to write these poems.

I want to acknowledge & thank the Lord for my children and grandchildren who faithfully serve the Lord & encourage me in my Send A Song Ministry, which now includes writing poetry.

Judy is very grateful to WLMB TV 40 for initiating my poem reading spots on our local Christian TV station!

ASK GOD FOR INSPIRATION

As I was sitting in God's creation
I prayed and asked God for inspiration
In the natural, the Lord will show
Something of spiritual value to know.

I saw two seeds blowing together
Not knowing where the wind would tether
When we scatter a seed of truth from our heart
The Spirit blows and spreads it apart.

One scatters here and the other there
His Word that we speak shows of God's care
We need to keep asking for God's inspiration
Walk in His ways: find interpretation.

All Scripture is given by inspiration of God, and is profitable
for doctrine, for reproof, for correction, for instruction in
righteousness, that the man of God may be complete, thoroughly
equipped for every good work.
II TIMOTHY 3:16 & 17

The entrance of Your Words gives light;
it gives understanding to the simple.
PSALM 119:130

JESUS IS CALLING YOU

With every sunrise and every sunset
You have a choice and will it be met.
Met with faith or melted with fear
Get into My Word, I see each tear.

My Word is supernatural
There's healing on its pages
Don't delay to read it;
Comfort for all stages.

I, the Lord, am calling you
To a higher way
Renew your mind daily
Then your heart will stay.

Whenever Satan tempted Me
I always spoke the Word
Daily come before Me
You'll know My voice you've heard.

Thy Word have I hid in mine heart, that I might not sin against Thee.
PSALM 119:11

I will delight myself in Thy statutes: I will not forget Thy Word.
PSALM 119:16

LOOK FOR MY LIGHT

Everyday is a decision,
You have to make a choice
Will you go your own way…
Or obey My gentle voice?

You look through the tunnel
To see My light….
If it wasn't for that
You'd be filled with fright.

You can't see My whole picture
But I have a wonderful plan
If you take the time to renew your mind
You'll be a happy man.

Just follow My footsteps
Do not be afraid…
My Word will guide you
'Til My full plan is stayed.

The Lord is my light and my salvation; whom shall I fear?
The Lord is the strength of my life; of whom shall I be afraid?
PSALM 27:1

And be not conformed to this world: but be ye transformed by
the renewing of your mind, that ye may prove what is that good,
and cceptable, and perfect, will of God.
ROMANS 12:2

DID I REFLECT YOUR SON

One thing I love on an evening so clear
Is to see the full moon, it seems so near.

We know that it is reflecting the sun
It lights up the sky when the day is done.

When my day is over, I usually pray
God did I finish your plan today?

Did I reflect your Son....
Or to my own ways did I run.

Please forgive if I neglected to stay
In Your presence to catch Your Son's ray.

There be many who say, Who will show us any good? Lord, Lift
Thou up the light of Thy countenance upon us.
PSALM 4:6

Thy Word have I hid in mine heart that I might not sin against
thee.
PSALM 119:11

GOD'S THOUGHTS OF ME

I wonder sometimes what
God thinks of me.
He thinks of me so often
Like the sands of the sea.

I love to see the ocean waves
Feel sand beneath my feet....
But nothing is more wonderful,
Or ever so sweet....

Than to know that God's thoughts of me
Are more than grains of sand....
Can't even comprehend the times
He reaches for my hand.

I want to please Him on my way
And by His side, I want to stay
Everyday I hope to pray,
Read His Word and then obey.

How precious also are Your thoughts to me, O God! How great
is the sum of them. If I should count them, they would be more
in number than the sand; when I awake, I am still with You.
PSALM 139:17, 18

HE HEARS EACH CRY

Soon little crocuses will be bursting thru the sod
Even through the snow flakes, created by our God.

They give us hope in winter that spring is coming soon
These flowers help us praise Him morning, night & noon.

When we are in a season, needing trust even more
God lets us know He's there, good will be in store.

He never will forsake us, He's always very near
He hears each cry and sees every tear.

These things I have spoken unto you, that in Me, ye might have
peace. In this world ye shall have tribulation: but be of good
Cheer: I have overcome the world.
JOHN 16:33

And they that know Thy name will put their trust in Thee: for
Thou Lord, hast not forsaken them that seek Thee.
PSALM 9:10

HE'LL DIRECT YOUR STEPS

The sun comes up the same every day
Twenty-four hours each has on his way.

Just like a camera with all of its takes
The things that I do, what a difference it makes.

Set your face like a flint, decide to follow
If not; in the mud, you might wallow.

Once a moment has passed; can't return
Must read God's Word to help me learn.

If I call out God's name in the morning light
He'll direct my steps before its night.

For the Lord God will help me; therefore I will not be disgraced;
Therefore, I have set my face like a flint. And I know that I will
not be ashamed.
ISAIAH 50:7

Trust in the Lord with all your heart, and lean not unto your own
understanding; in all your ways acknowledge Him and He will
direct your paths.
PROVERBS 3:5, 6

HE'LL HELP YOU LEARN

Under a tree looking up at the sky
Watching the birds with all freedom fly by
Why do we worry and why do we fret,
The Lord has never forsaken us yet.

He said He'd be there through
Thick and through thin…..
Just open your heart and let Jesus in.

Let Him take all of your care and concern
Open the Bible, He'll help you learn.
Inside its pages you'll find direction
He's waiting there with His awesome connection.

Open my eyes, that I may see wondrous things from your law.
PSALM 119:18

Teach me, O Lord, the way of Your statutes, and I shall keep it
to the end.
PSALM 119:33

HE'LL HELP YOU STAND

If you seek God's kingdom first
He'll make a way for you....
If you ask help to do His will
He'll be there to do.

If you don't trust
In your own plan....
He'll be there
To help you stand.

To the Lord confess your sin
It's the best thing you could do
God sent Jesus to die on a cross
He did it just for you.

Don't' stop there, He's wanting more
To others tell His story....
It will bring you joy and
Point them to God's glory.

It is God who girds me with strength, and makes my way perfect.
PSALM 18:32

I will call upon the Lord, Who is worthy to be praised: so shall I
be saved from my enemies.
PSALM 18:3

I KNOW THAT I CAN MAKE IT

Thank you Lord, for courage
That you put within my heart,
Thank you Lord, for patience
Only You can do that part.

I can even thank you, Lord
As trials come my way....
They come to make me strong
To prepare for heavens' stay.

You can make all things
Work out for my good,
I know that I can make it
Because You've understood.

My brethren, count it all joy, when you fall into various trials,
Knowing that the testing of your faith produces patience. But
let patience have its perfect work, that you may be perfect and
complete lacking nothing.
JAMES 1:2-4

I will be glad and rejoice in Thy mercy; for Thou hast considered
my trouble; Thou hast known my soul in adversities;
PSALM 31:7

I RELY ON YOU, LORD

Lord my hands are lifted to You
Why do I fret and why do I stew.
When worry comes, it hurts my heart
I know You're there to heal each part.

Unto the hills, I lift my eyes
You are there to hear my heart's cries
I rely on You, Your strength is there
Always ready to relieve each care.

I know that trials will surely come
If I count each one, it's quite a sum.
I know they come to make me strong
They teach me how to keep from wrong.

I will lift mine eyes unto the hills, from whence cometh my help.
My help cometh from the Lord, which made Heaven & earth.
PSALM 121:1, 2

The Lord is my rock, and my fortress, and my deliverer; my
God, my strength, in whom I will trust; my buckler, and the
horn of my salvation, and my high tower.
PSALM 18:2

I SENT MY SON

Obedience is everything in My plan
My hands of justice are not that of man.

When you sin, there is a consequence
My plan's forgiveness, true recompense.

I sent My son to die for you....
If you really love Me, you'll want to be true.

True to My Word, to walk in My way
Seeking to read in My presence each day.

In My Word, is the fragrance of life
There My presence dispels all the strife.

So sing My praises from morning 'til night
I will be there to help you do what is right.

If we confess our sins, He is faithful and just to forgive us our
sins, and to cleanse us from all unrighteousness.
1 JOHN 1:9

Let the wicked forsake his way, and the unrighteous man his
thoughts: and let him return unto the Lord, and He will have
mercy upon him; and to our God, for He will abundantly pardon.
ISAIAH 55:7

I'M THE GOD WHO KNOWS YOUR PATH

You think trials come way too often
Ask of Me; the blows to soften
I'm the God who knows Your path
Don't get bitter or give into wrath.

Just like palm trees planted in a row
Think of an arrow and a bow....
You are like an arrow, sent forth for Me
Trials come to make you strong, you see.

One step daily side by side
Trust in Me to be your guide
I know the way, just follow Me
You may be blind, but I can see.

I can see what lies ahead
Do not fear or dread
I am the God who's always in
And I will keep you from within.

You will show me the path of life, in Your presence is fullness of
joy; at your right hand are pleasures for evermore.
PSALM 16:11

Teach Me Your way, O, Lord, and lead Me in a path, because of
mine enemies.
PSALM 27:11

IN MY WORD THERE'S BLESSINGS

Why do you let fear come in
When you know that I'm with you
Why do you get short on faith
And begin to fret and stew.

Don't you know I'm with you
And I'm looking for a reason
One that shapes and molds
And helps in every season.

The seasons you go through in life
Have a specific plan
So don't give in to unbelief
Doubt or fear of man.

I want you to be close to Me
To help with every need
In My Word, there's blessing
If you truly heed.

Open Thou mine eyes, that I may behold wondrous things out
of Thy law.
PSALM 119:18

Thy Word is very pure: therefore thy servant loveth it.
PSALM 119:140

JESUS OUR LIGHTHOUSE

I love to see a Lighthouse, when I look across the lake
It gives me a security, that the storm cannot take.

The storm can't fill my heart with unrelenting fear....
For I will surely keep God's Lighthouse so very near.

His Word is the Lighthouse that calms my fearful heart
It covers and conquers the deepness of each part.

Keep looking up, when the storm is raging
Sing His praises and be engaging.....

Engage in prayer and helping others
You sow and you reap from sisters and brothers.

The Lord is my light and my Salvation; whom shall I fear? The
Lord is the strength of my life; of whom shall I be afraid?
PSALM 27:1

Remember Your Word unto Your servants, upon which You
have caused me to hope.
PSALM 119:49

LITTLE THINGS CAN BOTHER US

One day while setting in the sun to study for a class
A bee came by disturbing me, crawled right from the grass.

It's funny how the little things can bother us a lot
They can pile up and make us feel tied in a knot.

Sometimes the things that bother us are just surface things
We must look deep within our heart and see what really stings.

We may be holding bitterness, worry, or fear
Ask the Lord's forgiveness, He will always hear.

Once your slate is clean and you can then be free
You'll find some things won't bother you, even a little bee.

If we confess our sins, He is faithful and just to forgive us our
sins and cleanse us from all unrighteousness.
I JOHN I: 9

Take us the foxes, the little foxes, that spoil the vines: for our
vines have tender grapes.
SONG OF SOLOMON 2:15

LOOK BEYOND YOURSELF

God has a plan for His creation
It's full of excitement and imagination.
How do you find God's way and God's will
Stay close to Him and climb the hill.

Don't stop climbing, reach for His hand
Look beyond yourself, He'll help you stand.
Stand on His Word, it never changes
It will guide your life, it ever arranges.

At times, you may not understand
But keep on trusting, He'll hold your hand.
Your days are numbered in every way
Stay close to Him, you will not stray.

When thou goest, it shall lead thee; when thou sleepest it shall
keep thee; and when thou awakest, it shall talk with thee. For
the commandment is a lamp and the law is light; and reproofs of
instruction are the way of life.
PROVERBS 6:22, 23

LORD, HELP US GIVE OUR LOVE

Early in the morning, sometimes in the dark
The birds begin their song, singing like a lark.

I love to hear them sing, but they can waken you from sleep
So at that early time, I wish their song, they'd keep.

Every human being, God creates a special way
Sometimes their sounds annoy us; it's at those times we pray.

Each bird has different sounds and sings at special seasons
Lord, help us give our love to others without apparent
reasons.

We never know what someone else may be going through
We can sing that song of grace, the Lord will help us, to.

Love worketh no ill to his neighbor; therefore love is the fulfilling
of the law.
ROMANS 13:10

A new commandment I give unto you, that ye love one another;
as I have loved you, that ye also love one another. By this shall
all men know that ye are my disciples, if ye have love one to
another.
JOHN 13:34, 35

GOD'S COMFORT

As the moon comes out at the end of day
Reflecting the sun along the way.
We can find God's comfort and His care
He meets you in darkness; He's always there.

Sometimes the night seems O, so long
Don't be discouraged.....
When we're weak, He's strong.

Our greatest witness might come when we're weak
Others see His grace and begin to seek....
They will seek and find that your strength is sure
You'll point them to Jesus, so they can endure.

And He said unto me, My Grace is sufficient for you; for my
strength is made perfect in weakness.
11 CORINTHIANS 12:9

This is my comfort in my affliction: for Thy Word hath quickened
me.
PSALM 119:50

GOD REMOVES HEAVY BANDS

Looking at My beauty
Your heart begins to melt....
Going through a hard place
My presence then is felt.

When you give your life to Me
And you surrender to My way....
You can feel Me in creation
Whether clouds or sun each day.

You do not understand
Why things happen as they do....
But you look to heaven
As I make a way for you.

I send help in many ways
Through my Word and other's hands
Take heart my precious child
I'll remove those heavy bands.

For Thou hast broken the yoke of his burden, and the staff of
his shoulder, the rod of his oppressor, as in the day of Midian.
ISAIAH 9:4

And ye shall know the truth, and the truth shall make you free.
If the Son therefore shall make you free, ye shall be free indeed.
JOHN 8:32, 36

GOD KNOWS THAT YOU ARE WEAK

Be careful what you say....
When your life is all but nice
Keep your heart pliable
With much of God's advice.

God allows a trail...
To come into your life
To see if you will trust Him
And give Him all your strife.

God's Word will perform
All that you need
Take time to pray...
His advice then to heed.

God knows that you are weak
So in His Word you'll seek....
He's the vine we're the branches
He'll give you strength to take some chances.

Therefore I take pleasure in infirmities, in reproaches, in needs, in persecutions, in distresses, for Christ's sake. For when I am weak, then I am strong.
II CORINTHIANS 12:10

GIVE HIM YOUR BURDENS

When life hurts and no answers come
You feel rejected and very lonesome.

Jesus cares about your hearts cry
You are the reason He came to die.

He's always there to look for the lost....
He'll do what it takes at any cost.

So give Him your heaviness; all of your heart
He will be there to heal every part.

His comfort is different than you could find
Give Him your burdens; He'll calm your mind.

He healeth the broken in heart, and bindeth up their wounds.
PSALM 147:3

I will not leave you comfortless: I will come to you.
JOHN 14:18

A CALMING SCENE

There are days we feel busy as bees
So much to do, God help us please.
And then we look into God's Book
Find peace and calm in every nook.

His Word is like a calming scene
Where robins sing and trees are green
If we take time to hear His voice
We'll surely be able to make the right choice.

I will be glad and rejoice in Thy mercy: for Thou hast considered
my trouble; Thou hast known my soul in adversities.
PSALM 31:7

The Lord will give strength unto His people; the Lord will bless
His people with peace.
PSALM 29:11

A THANKFUL HEART

When the Lord created trees, He had a plan in mind
He thought of our enjoyment, He is a God who's kind

He brings out His paintbrush in the Fall
The leaves are so beautiful from Oak Trees tall.

Reds, greens and golds, so brilliant we see….
It is so amazing how he made each tree.

They glow even brighter, when the sun is out
With a thankful heart, we just want to shout.

Shout His praises to the highest hill
Thanksgiving is a choice, an act of the will.

When you open your eyes in the morning each day
Be sure to thank God as you begin to pray.

Enter His gates with thanksgiving, and into His courts with
praise, be thankful to Him and bless His name.
PSALM 100:4

Let us come before His presence with thanksgiving, let us shout
joyfully to Him with psalms.
PSALM 95:2

A GRATEFUL HEART IN TROUBLE

When dark clouds come with rolling thunder
It seems at times to put us under.....
The shock of news you weren't expecting
On your knees; in prayer connecting.

Always believe that the sun will peek through
During the storm, God, was there, too.
A grateful heart will help see the light
Praising the Lord, in your darkest night.

God has a way of using your trial
If you give it to Him, He'll help you smile.
His ways are higher than any of yours.....
His Word will help you to use His powers.

My Brethren, count it all joy when you fall into divers temptations;
knowing this, that the trying of your Faith worketh patience.
But let patience have her perfect work, that you may be perfect
and entire wanting nothing.
JAMES 1:2-4

Be careful for nothing; but in everything by prayer and supplication
with thanksgiving let your requests be made known unto God.
And the peace of God which passeth all understanding shall
keep your hearts and minds in Christ Jesus.
PHILIPPIANS 4:6, 7

TRUST IN THE LORD

The ocean waves are beautiful, refreshing and free
Giving us joy as we walk by the sea.

But then there are times that the waves are crashing
Bringing us fear with their roaring and thrashing.

When Jesus is near and says, "Peace be still."
All we can do is ask for His will.

Sometimes He will calm us in our storm....
Other times He will turn it from its form.

Our timing is different in every way
Trust in the Lord for the battle each day.

Though I walk in the midst of trouble, thou wilt revive me;
Thou wilt stretch forth thine hand against the wrath of mine
enemies and Thy right hand shall save me.
Psalm 138:7

Fear thou not, for I am with thee; Be not dismayed, for I am thy
God. Yea I will strengthen thee, Yea I will help thee, Yea I will
uphold thee with the right hand of My righteouness.
Isaiah 41:10

AN OBJECT LESSON JUST FOR ME

We were outside in God's lovely creation
It speaks to me encouragement and imagination.

Right beside my chair, a little ways away
Was a cute little gecko taking a long stay.

He started doing push-ups: four in a row
He waited a long time, didn't move, and didn't go.

It was so unusual; I knew that God was talking
An object lesson just for me, to help in my life's walking.

When we face a storm, our spirit exercises
Then we wait on God and His help soon arises.

If we take the time to notice, there are signs everywhere
God shows us things in nature about His loving care.

But they that wait on the Lord shall renew their strength; they
shall mount up with wings as eagles; they shall run and not be
weary; and they shall walk, and not faint.
ISAIAH 40:31

My soul, wait thou only upon God; for my expectation is from
Him.
PSALM 62:5

STINKING THINKING

Two weeks in a row, I was encountered by a stink bug
In our car, in a store & finally on our rug.

Don't ever smash a stink bug, for very soon you'll know
The reason for its name will surely make a show.

Then the next Sunday morning, our pastor gave a sermon
If I didn't hear it then, he might as well speak German.

He talked on "Stinking Thinking," as I squirmed in my seat
The Lord put the light on and turned up the heat.

I knew in my heart, I was giving in to worry...
I asked God's forgiveness and did it in a hurry.

Hurry to help me Lord, remove stinking thinking
I'm really aware now, from it I will be shrinking.

Thou wilt keep him in perfect peace, whose mind is stayed on
Thee: because he trusteth in thee.
ISAIAH 26:3

Cast all your care upon Him; for He careth for you.
I PETER 5:7

TOGETHERNESS

Togetherness is a powerful thing
A marvelous strength is what it can bring.

When others are in the valley of life
Our love can bring them help in the strife.

Our prayers make them feel like others are there
It is like God's arms around them with care.

So walk in the Spirit, be there for others
God will bless you through sisters and brothers.

Two are better than one; because they have a good reward for
their labor. For if they fall, the one will lift up his fellow: but
woe to him who is alone when he falls; for he has not another
to help him up.
ECCLESIASTES 4:9, 10

We took sweet counsel together, and walked into the house
Of God in company.
PSALM 55:14

WHEN GOD SAYS NO

How do you react when God says, "No"
Do you keep on trusting and continue to show….

To show that you are willing to stand strong and tall
Be able to resist when Satan comes to call.

It's at those times of death or loss, or doubts we are aware
If you remain faithful, He'll help with every care.

So, don't become angry, when you don't get your way
You will grow in times of loss, it can happen day by day.

Renew your mind daily, in the Word, my friend
He will guide your life, right until the very end.

The grass withers, the flower fades, but the Word of our God
shall stand forever.
ISAIAH 40:8

My soul melts for heaviness: strengthen Thou me according
unto Your Word.
PSALM 119:28

WE REACH OUT TO YOU

O, Lord, as the sun rises every day
We reach out to You in a special way.

We don't know the final end of things
But we trust in You and what it brings.

Our hearts are depending in Your Word and prayer
We know we can believe in Your healing care.

You died on a cross to free us from sin
Take my life; open my heart; please come in.

I want to serve You the rest of my life
I know with Your help it will calm every strife.

Jesus Christ the same yesterday, and to-day, and forever.
HEBREWS 13:8

Heal me, O Lord, and I shall be healed; save me, and I shall be
saved: for Thou art my praise.
JEREMIAH 17:14

WAIT ON THE LORD

What does it mean to wait on the Lord...
Praying together in one accord.
When the disciples waited in the upper room
Great things happened which dispelled much gloom.

What happened after praying
Changed the course of history
The Holy Spirit began to move
That's still a mystery.

Take that special time
To do some connecting
It will change your course of history....
So don't be neglecting.

When Jesus ascended into heaven
A helper He would send....
Because of victory on the cross,
The Holy Spirit now will mend.

If we take time to wait on Him,
And put out all distractions....
The Spirits there with mighty power
Better than all attractions.

Wait on the Lord; Be of good courage, and He will strengthen
thine heart. Wait, I say on the Lord.
PSALM 27:14

You have made known to me the ways of life; You will make me
full of joy in Your presence.
ACTS 2:28

WHILE WE WAIT

Waiting is so hard to do
Only the Lord can help us through.
We're on the other side of the gate
Looking through; He's never late.

Our prayers have been sent to His listening ear
We believe that He's always near.
We've read how trials make us strong
While we wait, He'll help us along.

In our special time of waiting
Be aware of the Devil's baiting.
Don't give in to doubt or fear
Our precious Lord is there to hear.

To hear our every longing call
He's there to keep us from a fall.
Let His love come from His voice
In His Word, we'll make the right choice.

I wait for the Lord, my soul doth wait, and in His Word, do I
hope.
PSALM 130:5

If any of you lack wisdom, let him ask of God, that giveth to
all men liberally, and upbraideth not; and it shall be given him.
JAMES 1:5

WHY THERE ARE MOUNTAINS

My mountains are so strengthening
I, the Lord would say…..
But there are things that trouble you
And questions come each day.

You don't know why your mountains
Could help to make you strong…..
It's only through My Word
That will make it all belong.

All things work together
If only you'll believe….
Stay very close to Me
And My wisdom you'll receive.

Father knows what's best for you
Don't try to work your plan….
It will only fail you see
For I am God, not man.

And we know that all things work together for good to them who love God, to them who are the called according to His purposes.
ROMANS 8:28

For as the Heavens are higher than the Earth, so are my ways higher than your ways, and my thoughts than your thoughts.
ISAIAH 55:9

WITH JESUS YOU'RE STRONGER

When I see a courthouse tower
With a clock ticking there....
It reminds me of God's justice
His love and His care.

If we obey God's commandments
And we do it with love.....
He will be there with help
And timing from above.

Many will not choose
To follow in God's way
Then justice will happen
They bring it on each day.

The time of life is short
Don't wait any longer
Be truly repentant
With Jesus, you are stronger.

I came not to call the righteous, but sinners to repentance.
LUKE 5:32

O man greatly beloved, fear not: peace be unto thee, be
strong, yea, be strong. And when he had spoken unto me, I
was strengthened, and said, Let my lord speak; for thou hast
strengthened me.
DANIEL 10:19

BE THANKFUL HOW GOD MADE YOU

See the snowflakes falling
Tumbling through the air
Every one is different
God made each one so rare.

Inspiration from creation
If we have an ear to hear
God has made us all unique
That is very clear.

Be thankful how God made you
Don't yearn to be another
It will only wear you out
Trying to be like your brother.

Use the gifts God's given you
They fit like a glove
God designed them just for you
Out of His great love.

For every creature of God is good, and nothing is to be refused
if it is received with thanksgiving; for it is sanctified by the word
of God and prayer.
I TIMOTHY 4:4

BE VERY WATCHFUL

When you look around God's time clock is there
Some choose to ignore it and live without a care.

Putting material things before the Lord
Much pleasure and things; want more to hoard.

The Bible warns us that in the last days
Lovers of self; our eyes filled with haze.

A haze that can blind us from the truth of God's Word
Be very watchful or deception is heard.

Don't be a statistic like the days of Noah….
If we are not careful, we'll be choked by a Boa.

Stay close to Jesus, don't follow the crowd
Get in God's Word and He'll speak very loud.

But the end of all things is at hand: be ye therefore sober and
watch unto prayer.
1 PETER 4:7

Now the Spirit speaks expressly that in the later times some
shall depart from the Faith, giving heed to seducing spirits and
doctrines of devils;
1 TIMOTHY 4:1

DARK CLOUDS

The dark clouds were forming in the sky
It was time to prepare, my heart's cry.

When life gets hard and times are rough
Call out to God, He's more than enough.

He wants to be there in every trial
He will help you; then give you a smile.

He's always looking out for our good....
Helps us to live in the way that we should.

We can't understand every way and plan
His Word helps us trust Him, not plans of man.

Stay close to Jesus and all will work out
Don't give in and be filled with doubt.

Jesus died to free us from sin
Open your heart and let His Word in.

Consider my affliction, and deliver me: for I do not forget Your
law. Plead my cause, and deliver me: quicken me according to
Your Word.
PSALM 119:153

You are my hiding place and my shield: I hope in your Word.
PSALM 119:114

MY MERCIES ARE NEW

My mercies are new every morning
As you wake to the brightness of sun
Take time to read My Word….
And then your day has begun.

You never know what a day may bring
But look to Me, the Brighter One
I have a plan that you don't understand
But pray My will to be done.

My ways are higher than yours
You may not see right away
Obey Me; the test of your faith….
Righteousness counted each day.

It is the Lord's mercies that we are not consumed, because His compassions fail not. They are new every morning: great is Your faithfulness.
LAMENTATIONS 3:22, 23

For My thoughts are not your thoughts, neither are your ways my ways, saith the Lord.
ISAIAH 55:8

Even as Abraham believed God, it was accounted to him for Righteousness.
GALATIANS 3:6

MY MAMMA READ EACH NIGHT

When I was but a little girl
I loved to hear a story…..
My mamma read each night to us
All about God's glory.

The magazine was called, "My Chum"
We gathered in when she said, "Come."
Mamma's stories that she would read….
If we took to heart; it helped with greed.

The stories gave us lessons
All about our choices….
We're to listen to God's Word,
Not to other voices.

Now that I am older
To my children I would say,
"Be sure to read those stories
From God's Word everyday.

Sanctify them by Your truth, Your Word is truth. As you sent
Me into the world, even so have I also sent them into the world.
And for their sakes I sanctify Myself, that they also might be
sanctified through the truth.
JOHN 17:17-19

My son, forget not My law; but let your heart keep My
commandments:For length of days, and long life, and peace,
shall they add to you.Let not mercy and truth forsake you: bind
them about your neck; write them upon the table of your heart:
So shall you find favour and good understanding in the sight of
God and man.
PROVERBS 3:1-4

BE PREPARED

I love to see a sail boat
It surely tells a tale…..
It calls for a wind
But never a gale.

When you decide to sail
You must always beware….
That a storm could come up
So you need to prepare.

So it is in your life
Don't wait 'til it's too late
Be prepared ahead of time
To fasten the gate.

Keep a portion of God's Word
Hidden deep in your heart
Then when storms come
You won't fall apart.

Hold on to each other
At times of fear….
God loves through others
He's always near.

I wait for the Lord, my soul doth wait, and in His Word do I hope.
PSALM 130:5

Our soul waiteth for the Lord: He is our help and our shield.
PSALM 33:20

PRAY AND THEN LET GO

What would we be like if we always got our way
If we never had a dark cloud, or a rainy day.
We may end up selfish and very shallow, too
God knows when to bring the clouds and how to take us
through.

So when things detain us, or plans go astray
Know if God allows it, trust He'll make a way.
When storm clouds form and the wind begins to blow
Stay close to Jesus; pray and then let go.

The name of the Lord is a strong tower: the righteous runneth
into it, and is safe.
PROVERBS 18:10

My soul melteth for heaviness: strengthen Thou me according
unto Thy Word.
PSALM 119:28

LORD, FILL MY CUP

Sometimes things seem twisted up
I ask the Lord to fill my cup.

Fill my cup, Lord, with Your peace
Take each wrinkle and each crease.

Press it out with verse so clear
That I'll trust You with each tear.

So much comfort I see there
Begin to read and find Your care.

The thirsting of my soul is quenched
When my heart is fully wrenched.

You put much joy within my cup
When die to self; keep looking up.

I will take the cup of Salvation, and call upon the name of the
Lord.
PSALM 116:13

My soul thirsts for God, for the living God: when shall I come
and appear before God?
PSALM 42:2

MUSIC TO MY EARS

You must think about the end of life
What it has in store.
When the days of life are over
And time shall be no more.

Will you go to heaven
And see Jesus face to face
Where the heavenly music sounds
Filling every space.

If hearing God's Word
Is like music to your ears
And obeying Him is what you love
Through laughter and through tears.

Then you will find contentment
In the midst of every trial
You'll lean on Jesus and
He'll be with you every mile.

Your testimonies I have taken as a heritage forever, for they are the rejoicing of my heart. I have inclined my heart to perform Your statutes forever, to the very end.
PSALM 119:111, 112

For He satisfies the longing soul, and fills the hungry soul with goodness.
PSALM 107:9

Judy and her older sister, Joyce, who went to heaven at 37 years old! We know that because she had accepted Jesus Christ as her Lord and Savior and was living for Him.

This is Judy's family, with her first husband Dean, who went to heaven at 67 years of age. They had 3 children, Tony, Beth & Aaron.

This is Judy with her 3 grown children, Tony, Beth & Aaron.

One of the loves of Judy's life, her 8 grandchildren, taken when she was a widow.

Judy with her siblings, Marty, Miriam, Jim & Bob.(Joyce & Evy are already in heaven)

The Lord brought a wonderful Christian man, the love of her life, Jim Hill, into Judy's life, this is their wedding day on Leap Year, 2/29/08.

Judy & Jim had a Big Vintage Family Wedding & this is their blended family!

Jim took Judy to Hawaii for their honeymoon...a much needed rest, after planning a big wedding in just 6 weeks! Waikiki Beach area was where they stayed.

Judy & Jim at Delray Beach, where they like to go in the winter. Notice the Gospel Tracts in Jim's pocket, they love to spread God's Word in Florida. Judy also gets much inspiration for her poetry there.

Jim & Judy both enjoy light houses; this one is in Ludington, MI.

Judy is recording her latest CD, "SEEK JESUS & FIND HIM." John Kuser (producer) and Judy are mixing the music at this point.

This is the cover of Judy's latest CD, "SEEK JESUS & FIND HIM."

This is the cover of Judy's recent CD, "HIS RIGHT HAND UPHOLDS ME."

Judy loves to read God's Word at the ocean, and take time to pray
& listen.

Judy expresses her thanks to the Lord for the beautiful sunrise that comes every morning along the ocean at Delray Beach, Fl.

Judy has been doing the Share-a-thons for WLMB TV 40 for 13 years. Jamey Schmitz, the CEO & President along with Jeff Millslagle, the Sr. VP of Operations/Program Director, are also helping to bring in the pledges for WLMB. Judy met Jim through WLMB, as he answers phones for pledges & prayers.

NEW HOPE

When the sun in the sky is very slight
And there's a foreboding darkness of night.

It's time to remember what My Word says to you
I'll never leave you; I'll make your heart new.

Wait upon Me in your darkest hour
I will come in with mighty power.

I will give you a Word in due season
I'm there for you, without a reason.

Remember it's darkest before the dawn
If you trust in my Word, new hope it will spawn.

Faithful is He that called you, who also will do it.
1 THESSALONIANS 5:24

Thou has dealt well with they servant, O Lord, according unto
Thy Word.
PSALM 119:65

OUR DARKEST TIMES

Dancing here and there is a pretty butterfly
He's free as can be flying in the sky.

But there was a time deep in the cocoon
It was an ugly creature, freedom was not soon.

If man tries to pry out the cocoon before it's ready
The butterfly may die, be damaged or unsteady.

It's at our darkest times God is working for our good
Inside our cocoon, we must know He's understood....

Understood our wonderings and our hearts cry
We must know our loving Father works things out by and by.

And we know that all things work together for good to those
who love God, to those who are called according to His
purpose. For Whom He did foreknow, He also did predestinate
to be conformed to the image of His Son, that He might be the
Firstborn among many brethren.
ROMANS 8:28

For I am persuaded, that neither death, nor life, nor Angels,
nor principalities, nor powers, nor things present, nor things to
come, nor height, nor depth, nor any other creature, shall be able
to separate us from the Love of God, which is in Christ Jesus
our Lord.
ROMANS 8:38, 39

OUR HEART WILL NOT BE HARDENED

The concrete truck; some lessons we might learn
It must be air tight, moving at every turn.

Preparation has been made for it's pouring out
The form is there, the workers give a shout.

If we keep moving close to Him and obey His direction
Our heart will not be hardened and we'll have a good
connection.

The Lord can then use us to do His kingdom work
If we keep our eyes on Jesus, and don't ever shirk.

But Jesus said to him, "No one, having put his hand to the plow,
and looking back, is fit for the kingdom of God.
LUKE 9:62

Beware brethren, lest there be in any of you an evil heart of
unbelief in departing from the living God; but exhort one
another daily while it is called, "Today," lest any of you be
hardened through the deceitfulness of sin.
HEBREWS 3:12, 13

PEACE WILL COME

When your eyes on Jesus are stayed
And on Him the price was paid.

Peace will come in your darkest hour
He is the one that has the power....

The power to see you through your testing
Just read His Word and find a resting.

So many voices may steer you wrong
Commune with God and you'll be strong.

Strong to stand against any trial
His Spirit will comfort and give you a smile.

Peace, I leave with you, My peace I give unto you; not as the
world giveth, give I unto you. Let not your heart be troubled,
neither let it be afraid.
JOHN 14:27

Lord, Thou wilt ordain peace for us: for Thou also hast wrought
all our works in us.
ISAIAH 26:12

SET YOUR FACE LIKE A FLINT

A beautiful day out the backdoor we went
Just beneath the door sill was a creature sent.

Awaiting his entry the sly gecko came
Intrudes in our room, never the same.

If we are not watchful, the devil slips in
Waiting to bring into clutches of sin.

Whatever you do, be strong in God's Word
Then you're prepared; His advice you've heard.

Set your face like a flint, don't give Satan an inch
Then you'll conquer sin, with God's help it's a cinch.

Yet in all things, we are more than conquerors through Him who
loved us.
ROMANS 8:37

My soul melts from heaviness; strengthen me according to Your
Word.
PSALM 119:28

TAKE GOD'S HAND

When trials come and you feel the weight
We remember days when we stayed out late.
We stayed beside the ocean breeze....
Felt God's hand and help with ease.

We cannot stay in life without pain
His hand is there, we feel His reign
He reigns in every storm and gale
He helps us with the set of sail.

Lord, help our mind to be content
Not to Satan, pay his rent.
When in Your Word, we find our heart
Then letting go, it's time apart.

It's time apart with no distractions
Hear His voice and interactions.
Kneel in prayer and then you're free
Take God's hand to clearly see.

And they that know Thy name will put their trust in Thee: for
Thou Lord, hast not forsaken them that seek Thee.
PSALM 9:10

You shall show me the path of life: in Your right hand there are
pleasures forevermore.
PSALM 16:11

TAKE TIME ON THE PORCH

Sitting on the porch, having our devotions
It surely helps a lot to control our emotions.

We don't want to miss spending time with God
He's there to guide with His staff and His rod.

When we make time for learning…..
It helps our deepest yearning.

If we don't seek His face….
We will not win the race.

He's the good shepherd who calls to His sheep
Take time on the porch His commandments to keep.

The Lord is my shepherd; I shall not want. He makes me to lie down in green pastures; He leads me beside still waters, He restores my soul; He leads me in the paths of righteousness for His name's sake. Yea, though I walk through the valley of the shadow of death, I will fear no evil: for You are with me; your rod and your staff they comfort me.
PSALM 23:1-4

And thine ears shall hear a word behind thee, saying, this is the way, walk ye in it, when ye turn to the right hand, and when ye turn to the left.
ISAIAH 30:21

THE LORD GAVE AN ANSWER

"The Lord is with you, O mighty man of valor,"
An angel spoke to Gideon not feeling very stellar.

The angel had a message to give from God
Gideon's mind was churning as he gave a nod.

Gideon was given a very hard task,
He wasn't sure what to do, so this is what he asked….

He put out two fleeces to see which way to go
The Lord gave an answer, surely He did show.

Because of his obedience, the battle was won
He wanted to be sure or he'd be undone.

Sometimes we're at a loss and we don't know what to do
The Lord will see our fleeces and bring us draught or dew.

The Word will confirm it and give you guidance , too
If your heart is filled with Jesus, all these things will work for you.

I will instruct thee and teach thee in the way which thou shalt go:
I will guide thee with mine eye.
PSALM 32:8

For the Lord will help me; therefore shall I not be confounded:
therefore have I set my face like a flint, and I know that I shall
not be ashamed.
ISAIAH 50:7

THE LORD UNDERSTANDS

Consider the lilies, they toil not nor spin
Father God cares for them always within.

At times we may doubt when our provision is slight
We find fear coming out in the midst of dark night.

The Lord understands and He's waiting each hour
His Word walks beside us, it gives us great power.

If we are obedient throughout all our days....
God will take care of us in all His kind ways.

If we stay close to Jesus and call Him our friend
He will watch over us to the very end.

Consider the lilies, how they grow: they neither toil nor spin; and
yet I say to you, even Solomon in all his glory was not arrayed
like one of these.
LUKE 12: 27, 28

The young lions do lack, and suffer hunger: but they that seek
the Lord shall not want any good thing.
PSALM 34:10

THE ROSE

My favorite flower is the rose
It stands stately & tall wherever it grows.

But be very careful, the thorns are there, too
If you're not; you'll find blood in the dew.

We must be prepared for thorns in our day
The Bible warns us, but He'll make a way.

God allows the thorns with that fragrant flower
He can help us beware with His mighty power.

His Word will equip us for battles each day
On our knees we find self to fade away.

Our selfish ways are like those thorns
We overcome, repentant we mourn.

If we confess our sins, He is faithful and just to forgive our sins,
and to cleanse us from all unrighteousness.
I JOHN 1:9

As far as the east is from the west, so far hath He removed our
transgressions from us.
PSALM 103:12

YOU WILL BE WISE

I will lift mine eyes to the hills
Is the first of Psalm one twenty-one...
The Psalm that my mother enjoyed
"Till her final day was done.

There's just something that happens
When upward we look....
It then makes us want to go to the Book.

The Book of life to find answers there
No other Book will give wisdom to share
Too much humanism can blind your eyes
Stay in God's Book and you will be wise.

I will lift up my eyes unto the hills, from whence comes my help.
My help comes from the Lord, which made heaven and earth.
PSALM 121:1-2

And from a child you have known the Holy Scriptures, which
are able to make you wise unto Salvation through faith which is
in Christ Jesus.
11 TIMOTHY 3:15

WE MAKE THE CHOICE

Unseasonable weather, how sweet it can be
Allowing you time; filled with glee....

But then comes the days that your heart might get sad
God allows bad days, so don't get mad.

He only allows things into your life
That will bring you closer to Him in the strife...

We make the choice to get bitter or better,
Lord, please help me with each fetter.

Guide me, Lord, is always my cry....
Help me choose wisely by and by.

My brethren, count it all joy, when you fall into various trials, knowing that the trying of your Faith works patience. But let patience have her perfect work, that you may be perfect and entire wanting nothing.
JAMES 1:2-4

PRAYER CHANGES THINGS

There's nothing like prayer to change your life
Call out to God to dispel all your strife.

Pray for others; pray for our nation
God will be there with revelation.

Confess your sin, God will forgive
Because of Jesus, He'll help you to live.

If you don't take time to communicate
Just like you do each day with your mate,

You grow apart, God seems far away
Ask God to help you, take time to pray.

He surely will do that, if it's truly your heart
If you do yours, He'll do His part.

The effectual fervent prayer of a righteous man availeth much.
JAMES 5:16

Evening and morning and at noon, I will pray, and cry aloud,
and He shall hear my voice.
PSALM 55:17

THE STORMS OF LIFE

The storms of life will come to all
Some are big and some are small
Storms can be physical or emotional
Each one is helped by God's devotional.

If we decide everyday, to devote ourselves to Him
We'll not be deceived by every new age whim.
Every resolve will surely be tested
With the Lord's help, we will be rested.

Rested and ready prepared for each storm
If you're in the world, that's not the norm.
So when the storms come and you're crawling out
Think of it as growing, don't give in or pout.

He'll be there to help whether death or destruction
Stay in His Word for deep instruction.
Peace and calming you'll find there
Don't give up while you find God's care.

Therefore humble yourselves under the mighty hand of God,
that He may exalt you in due time.
I PETER 5:6

The Lord is good, a strong hold in the day of trouble; and He
knoweth them that trust in Him.
NAHUM 1:7

THIS COULD BE THE YEAR

Another year has ended, what's the New Year have in store
If we didn't know our Savior, we would deal with fear much more.

We know He holds the future and we're the apple of His eye
He'll help us with our trials and He will hear our cry.

It seems there's judgment in the land and uncertainty is there
If we obey His Word, He will answer every care.

This could be the year that Jesus comes for His believers
Make sure you know the counterfeit and don't believe deceivers.

This know also, that in the last days perilous times shall come.
11 TIMOTHY 3:1

But evil men and seducers shall wax worse and worse, deceiving and being deceived.
11 TIMOTHY 3:13

A NEW YEAR: NO FEAR

A new year has begun, a time to seek God's face
Get our marching orders to keep with in God's pace.

We need to stay connected, there is no other way
He'll show us what to do; He'll guide us day by day.

The things that happen in this year might bring our heart's to
fear
But when we're close to Jesus, He'll wipe away each tear.

Read God's Word and listen, He speaks on every page
It will calm your fear when you see the heathen rage.

In God have I put my trust: I will not be afraid what man can
do unto me.
PSALM 56:11

Pease I leave with you, my peace I give unto you: not as the
world give, give I unto you. Let not your heart be troubled,
neither let it be afraid.
JOHN 14:27

CPSIA information can be obtained at www.ICGtesting.com
Printed in the USA
BVOW032033180413

318426BV00001BB/89/P